ABC
ALBUQUERQUE BERNALILLO COUNTY
LIBRARIES

Donated in
Memory of
Mr. Richard A.
Freedman

# Learn Twitter in 10 Minutes

# Learn Twitter
# in 10 Minutes

The quickest way to learn to tweet

Lynn C Schreiber

**BATSFORD**

First published in the United Kingdom in 2012 by
Batsford, 10 Southcombe Street, London W14 0RA

An imprint of Anova Books Company Ltd

ISBN 978 1 84994 068 9
A CIP catalogue record for this book is available
from the British Library.

18  17  16  15  14  13  12
10  9  8  7  6  5  4  3  2  1

Reproduction by Mission Productions Ltd, Hong Kong
Printed and bound by 1010 Printing International Ltd, China

# Contents

Welcome to Twitter! It looks a bit confusing, doesn't it? It is actually very simple – take ten minutes to read this book and you'll see for yourself.

Twitter was founded in 2006 and within a year 400,000 tweets were posted each quarter. Fast-forward three years and 50 million tweets were posted in a day, and by 2012 an incredible 400 million messages a day were being tweeted.

Twitter was initially used by private individuals to share status updates, but soon the true strength of the network was realized: companies use it to reach out to their customers, governments use it to reach out to their citizens, and activists use it to organize campaigns and spread awareness.

# Getting started

Your first impression of Twitter might be the feeling of reading several disjointed conversations, peppered with strange abbreviations and symbols, but fear not, this is about to change!

When you first visit Twitter – at www.twitter.com – you will be asked to sign up, giving your name, an email address and a password.

When you click 'Sign up for Twitter' you will be directed to a registration page that features the details you have given, a suggested Username (your '@' name) that is a variation on the names you have provided, and other suggestions for Usernames you might prefer. If you don't like any of Twitter's Username suggestions, you can pick any name you like, but as there are so many Twitter users it might take a while before you find a good name that has not already been taken.

Remember that other people will be able to find you by name, Username or email address, although the latter will not be shown publicly, and you can disable this option later.

You can make one, both or neither of your Twitter names your real name. Try to make your Username as short as possible, to leave more space for tweeting, and also make it memorable and eye-catching. If you choose a generic-sounding name, such as '@tracey1974', then this might make it difficult for people searching for you.

On this page you will also find links to the terms of Service and Privacy Policy. Although these are long, boring and full of legal-type jargon, it is worth having a look so you know what you are signing up for!

Once you have signed up there is a tutorial to get you started. First this will make suggestions about people and organizations you might want to follow, and then it will ask you for your profile.

Add a bio to your profile so that your potential followers know something about you. Be funny or be serious, but be brief – you have just 160 characters to advertise yourself, but make the most of all of them. If you think of Twitter as a giant search engine, then your bio should contain key search words that define you (and help like-minded people to find you) and should also give a sense of the person you are.

> **@samplebio**
> Optimistic freelance writer/editor. Riesling quaffer, biscuit botherer, Twitter wrangler. Enthusiastic blogger and frequent political ranter.

As well as these details, be brave and add a photo. If you are shy, then a photo of scenery or a blog logo will do, but in general people respond better to a face – don't leave the Twitter egg as it marks you as a novice.

Adding a photo is easy. On the Twitter website, locate the small grey camera icon at the bottom left-hand corner of the text box in which you write your tweets: click to open your files, choose a photo, and voilà!

Your 'timeline' is the stream of tweets from people you follow. Now you are ready to find some folk to follow and fill that timeline.

Twitter is all about information and communication: you can tell people what you are doing or thinking and find out what other individuals/companies/ organizations are up to.

# Friends
## and
## followers

# Following folk

When you sign up, Twitter suggests people for you to follow. These are usually celebrities or prolific Twitter users. Twitter verifies the accounts of famous people, so make sure there is a little blue tick next to the name.

Just following celebrities can be boring, as they seldom follow back or reply to a tweet, so have a look for ordinary people to follow. Use the search box to find those tweeting about issues or hobbies that interest you, for example, rugby, physics or a genre of music you are keen on. Check out the profile and previous tweets of those people, and if they look particularly interesting, follow them – which goes to show how important it is to create an interesting profile.

If you regularly read a newspaper, blog or magazine online, you can follow it on Twitter by clicking on the 'Follow Me' button on their website. You can search for your favourite journalists and writers, who are often more likely to respond to their followers than celebrities. And if you have a favourite shop, restaurant or other business, you can follow it for special offers and news about its products.

# Finding followers

We all start with zero followers. Some people will go on to have thousands of followers, while others have only a handful. This should have no bearing on your enjoyment of Twitter: surely it is better to have 50 followers who share your interests, and reply to your tweets, than 5,000 followers who lurk silently and never communicate with you.

When you start to follow people, they will receive an email informing them of a new follower. Once you start chatting to them, some will follow you back; if they don't, it is nothing personal, so don't be offended. Resist the temptation to ask them why, or beg them to follow you – it will only make you sound desperate!

Watch out for spambots, which are accounts created in order to advertise a product, or direct you to a particular website that may contain material that you might find offensive, or might harbour a nasty virus waiting to attack your computer. If a spambot looks suspicious, be careful not to click on any links, and have a look at its previous tweets to see if it tweets the same thing to everyone. Clicking on a link may enable it to hack your account, so keep well clear. Always block and report to keep Twitter safe for everyone.

# First tweets

First of all, don't be shy. Twitter is made for dialogue, not monologue, and there is no such thing as interrupting a private conversation, although if you don't already know the other users it is polite to start your tweet with 'Sorry to butt in' or similar.

Twitter limits you to 140 characters, so you may have to be creative if you are usually fairly verbose. Try not to resort to text speak as not everyone understands it well.

# Tell us what is going on in your life

**Bill Boring** @boringtweeter
Eating eggs for breakfast.

(This is what most non-Twitterers think that Twitter users do, but in reality it might be slightly more interesting.) Everyone who follows you can see this.

# Reply to a tweet

**Lynn Schreiber** @LynnCSchreiber
@boringtweeter Boiled or fried?

Either hit the reply button, or type @ at the beginning to address that person, but be aware that those who follow both you and the person you are addressing will also see the tweet.

# Mention someone else

Put an @ in the middle of a tweet and everyone who follows you will see the tweet, not just those who also follow the person you are addressing.

**Lynn Schreiber** @LynnCSchreiber
Did you see that @boringtweeter is having eggs for breakfast?

(Note the different names and Usernames of Bill Boring and Lynn Schreiber, as explained on page 10.)

When replying to a tweet, another way of ensuring that people who follow both you and the person you are addressing will see your tweet is to put a full stop at the beginning, which in effect converts the tweet into a mention rather than a reply:

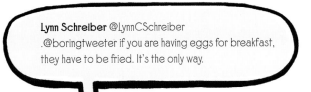

**Lynn Schreiber** @LynnCSchreiber
.@boringtweeter if you are having eggs for breakfast, they have to be fried. It's the only way.

This opens the conversation to anyone who follows you:

**Paul Poacher** @PoachedEgg
@boringtweeter @LynnCSchreiber Fried egg? That is just wrong. Why waste a good egg on a frying pan, when you could poach it?

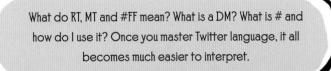

What do RT, MT and #FF mean? What is a DM? What is # and how do I use it? Once you master Twitter language, it all becomes much easier to interpret.

# Advanced tweeting

# How to retweet

Retweeting (RT for short) is used to pass on a tweet to your followers. It may be that you enjoyed the linked article, or the tweet was so funny/horrifying/offensive that you want your followers to read it too.

You can retweet without adding a comment, but this generally implies that you agree with the comment that you are retweeting.

# Retweeting and adding a comment

If you use a Twitter 'client' (see page 44) or a Twitter mobile phone app, you can add a comment to a RT.

**Bill Boring** @boringtweeter
RT @LynnCSchreiber I like eggs for breakfast.
<< me too, they are yummy

**Bill Boring** @boringtweeter
RT @LynnCSchreiber This is my favourite recipe for Eggs Benedict www.eggstraordinaryrecipe.com << looks delicious.

# Modified tweets

Sometimes you may want to change a tweet slightly, shorten it so that you can add your comment, or correct a spelling mistake. The use of MT for 'modified tweet' shows that the original tweet was slightly different.

**Lynn Schreiber** @LynnCSchreiber
This is my favourite recipe for Eggs Benedict, the absolute best way to prepare eggs, even if a bit time-consuming www.eggstraordinaryrecipe.com

**Bill Boring** @boringtweeter
MT @LynnCSchreiber This is my favourite recipe for Eggs Benedict, the absolute best way to prepare eggs www.eggstraordinaryrecipe.com

# Quoting tweets

You might also sometimes see a tweet quoted using quotation marks.

> **Bill Boring** @boringtweeter
> "@LynnCSchreiber This is my favourite recipe for Eggs Benedict, the absolute best way to prepare eggs www.eggstraordinaryrecipe.com" < looks good

Be brave and add your opinion when you retweet or quote tweets, as this encourages others to respond to you, and may net you some new followers.

But don't overdo the retweeting. A timeline full of retweeted comments and links is unlikely to persuade a potential follower to click that magic Follow button.

# Recommending links

You can also pass on a link or story and credit the person who first tweeted it:

Bill Boring @boringtweeter
This is a great website
www.eggstraordinaryrecipe.com (via @LynnCSchreiber)

# 'Favouriting' tweets

The 'Favourite' button allows you to bookmark tweets that you want to read again later, when you have more time. It is also handy if you don't have time to reply but want to remind yourself to comment on a tweet later.

# Hashtags (#)

A hashtag or '#' is a way of collating information about a particular topic. Use a hashtag before key words or phrases to make them easier to find. This can range from a television show, e.g. #xfactor, to a sporting event such as, #olympics or #worldcup. Don't overdo it with hashtags – one or two are enough in any one tweet.

Hashtags have been used during important world events such as elections and revolutions – the Arab Spring hashtags, such as #egypt, #jan25 and #egyelection, are particularly good examples of how hashtags can help to collate information.

Hashtags are also used for humorous or ironic effect, for example in tweets like, 'I went to the dentist today #ow' or 'Making the most of my day off #sittingarounddoingnothing'.

# Trending

When something is trending, it is one of the most talked-about topics on Twitter, often collated by using a #hashtag. Trending topics can be ridiculous, such as #ilovemydog, or world-changing, such as the Arab Spring hashtags, or an important national event like #GeneralElection. You can check what is trending both nationally and internationally.

Twitter allows companies to pay for sponsored tweets, which results in artificially trending topics, though these are clearly marked.

Twitter tailors your trends, so you see trends based on your location and followers. To see worldwide or country-based tweets, click the #Discover tag on web-based Twitter.

# Follow Friday

#FF is short for #FollowFriday, a Twitter trend created back in 2009 by Twitter users that has since become a customary Friday activity. Each Friday you can recommend Twitter profiles that you appreciate and enjoy to all of your followers, the idea being that your #FF recommendation will encourage others to check out that profile, generating more followers for them.

Don't just list five people in one tweet, or, even worse, use a #FF helper to pluck several random people from your follow list. Instead, tell your followers why you are recommending that they follow the person.

**Paul Poacher** @poachedegg
#ff @boringtweeter for not living up to his name

# Direct messages

A DM or 'direct message' is a tweet sent privately. You can only send a DM if you and the person you are messaging follow each other. A word of warning: don't set up an automatic DM to thank people for following you, as it can be viewed as spam and may get you swiftly unfollowed.

There is a wide range of third-party software 'apps' available to help you manage your Twitter feed.

# Little Twitter helpers

# Lists

After a while, you may be following so many people that your timeline moves too fast for you to keep up with it. This is where lists come in handy. Categorize those you follow into groups, e.g. 'work', 'news', 'fun', 'people for chatting', 'knitters', 'rugby tweeps', etc. (More Twitter lingo – 'tweep' is a shortened version of 'Twitter and 'Peeps', so a rugby tweep is someone that follows rugby on Twitter.) You can share these lists or keep them private.

Flicking back and forth between lists on the Twitter website can be slightly annoying, so now is a good time to look into different Twitter clients that enable you to see your lists at a glance.

# Twitter clients

Software that was developed to host Twitter accounts called 'Twitter clients' enable you to switch between several Twitter accounts, e.g. business and private, often in columns across your computer screen. Tweetdeck and Hootsuite are popular, but they update and change constantly, so ask your followers for their current recommendation.

# Mobile Twitter apps

The sheer brilliance of Twitter becomes most apparent when it is used on the go. Download one of the many apps on to your phone or tablet, and tweet whenever you have a spare minute. Whether under the table at a boring meeting, on public transport (check out #tubetweets) or when waiting for a friend to turn up, with Twitter on your phone you are never alone.

# Apps for clever stuff

There are lots of apps available to help you enhance your Twitter experience. These change almost daily, but here are some of the main functions you'll be able to find apps for.

# Twitter photos

There are various apps for sharing photos. Check them out and find which one suits you best.

# Deleting tweets

If you have shared more than you feel comfortable with, you can delete tweets up to a specified date with www.tweetdelete.net.

# Tracking followers

For keeping up to date with your follower list and seeing who unfollowed you, check out who.unfollowed.me – but remember not to take it personally!

A word of warning – don't use too many apps, and remove them later if you don't need them to protect your account from hackers.

The issue of privacy on social networking sites is a serious one: make sure you understand what you are using Twitter for and how far you need to protect yourself.

# Privacy

If you are using your own name, remember that everything you tweet can come back and haunt you. Deleting a tweet does not delete retweets, which may go on to be retweeted themselves. A disclaimer stating that the views expressed are your own and not those of your employer is a good idea, but this may not protect you completely. Be aware that anyone can sign up to Twitter and follow you.

Don't tweet anything that you are not prepared to defend. If you make a mistake, or inadvertently offend someone, apologise and move on.

Discussion and arguments are a part of Twitter, but if someone crosses the line you can block him or her from reading or commenting on your tweets. You can also report a Twitter user if his or her behaviour strays from being offensive to being illegal.

# Account settings

You can lock your account for added privacy, meaning that anyone who wishes to follow you will have to ask you first. Some people are reticent about sending a follow request to a locked account, so if you choose this option, be aware that you may not be able to build followers quite so easily.

# Trolls

Trolls are Internet users who deliberately post inflammatory comments in order to provoke a reaction. If you suspect someone is trolling, ignore or block him or her. It is always best not to engage with trolls.

# Using Twitter for business

- Don't do it half-heartedly: this is not a job for the office junior, just because she is young and will understand this new-fangled Twitter thing. Rather it is a project for an employee or agency who understands your brand, knows your products and how to sell them, and is able to check the Twitter account regularly throughout the day.

- Do it with humour: allow whoever is responsible to communicate openly and warmly with your customers, instead of behaving like a corporate robot.

- Post regularly: nothing turns a customer off more than a Twitter account that hasn't been updated for weeks.

- Set up a standard Twitter search for mentions of your product so that you can respond to anyone talking about them.

- Remember that you cannot control Twitter, as some well-known companies have found to their detriment. When a derogatory Twitter #hashtag is created by disgruntled customers, it is referred to as a 'bashtag'.

Here are some dos and don'ts for Twitter users so you can maximize your fun and your number of followers.

# How to make the most of Twitter

# Do

- Be polite and helpful.

- Reply when someone @mentions you.

- Give credit when you retweet – passing off someone else's jokes as your own is a big no-no.

- Thank others for retweeting your tweets and for #FF (but don't do a mass thanks for #FF).

- Remember basic Internet safety rules.

- If you are not sure of something, just ask. There will always be someone around to help you out.

# Don't

- Be taken in by 'Get More Followers' schemes or groups. Follow people because you are interested in what they have to say, not to amass thousands of followers.

- Only follow celebrities, most of whom don't reply.

- Use an app to find out who unfollowed you, and then ask them why.

- Just use Twitter to link to your blog or website, without interacting with your followers.

- Give up after a day, saying 'Boring!' Like so many things, you will get out what you put in, so persevere!

# Five fab things about Twitter

1. Watching TV becomes a social event when your timeline is full of people discussing the programme you are watching.

2. Finding the answer to an obscure question takes minutes of interaction with real people, instead of hours of Internet searching.

3. Keeping up to date with news and gossip is as easy as one-two-tweet.

4. When it is your birthday, your timeline is filled with good wishes and virtual pints of beer/glasses of wine.

5. Twitter knows no borders. You can exchange sushi recipes with a tweep in Japan, talk to an American about car racing, then ask an Australian for barbecue tips. All without leaving your armchair!

Right, your ten minutes are up – are you ready to go and share your thoughts in 140 characters and find out what's trending?

Off you go and happy tweeting!

# Glossary/index